LIFE AS A GEEZER

LIFE AS A GEEZER

by

Phil Batt

To TIFEDA —
Best Wishes!
Phil Batt
2011

ISBN 0-9677135-3-6

Additional Copies:
Contact
Eva Gay Yost
2638 N. Sea Cove Way
Meridian, Idaho 83642

DEDICATION

To Jacque, who has traveled with me on a long, exciting, occasionally bumpy, but wonderful trail. We've together become transformed from the young sweethearts who eloped, to the Geezer and Geezara who are now in their 55th year of marriage. Thanks for the trip.

Contents

Contents

ACKNOWLEDGEMENTS

To Eva Gay Yost – a Jack (Jill)–of-all-trades. She is my scheduler, typist, proof-reader and advisor. Most of her advice is designed to keep me out of trouble and to protect my privacy. For this I'm deeply indebted.

And to Lindy High. Lindy was my speech writer when I was Governor. She is absolutely tops as a sharp-eyed grammarian, and wrote her own highly successful column for many years. She kindly consented to proofing and correcting this effort, just as she did for "The Compleat Phil Batt."

LIFE AS A GEEZER

FOREWORD

I lost a close gubernatorial election to John Evans in November 1982. In the winter of 1984 Jacque and I made a tour of southern Arizona with an eye toward a wintertime haven. Our farm duties were not confining during the cold months. At that time I had no further interest in politics. We were not interested in the glamour of California and thought South Texas to be a little remote; therefore we turned our attention to Arizona.

We took a good look at Green Valley, a town of 15,000 inhabitants 20 miles south of Tucson and 1100 miles south of Boise. It was peopled mostly by elderly snowbirds. Large sections of Green Valley were restricted to those who had been born at least 55 years ago. The average age was 70½ years. We liked the area a lot but thought that there were too many old Geezers, elderly wives and widows living there. After all, we hadn't reached that golden milestone of 60 yet.

We went back again a few years later. We had attained the three score mark. Although we hardly felt old, we had our AARP cards and were shamelessly enjoying the age discounts offered by hundreds of establishments for no good reason.

We bought a winter townhouse shortly thereafter and have spent a lot or a little time in Arizona each year since. Our annual tenure there was severely curtailed when I plunged back into politics. Now that I have forsaken such activity, Green

Valley is our winter home. In the meantime I have become a Geezer myself. The average age in Green Valley has risen to 71, but now I'm one of the elders at 75. While the number of permanent residents has more than doubled, Green Valley has yet to be stifled by overpopulation.

Life as a Geezer is interesting to say the least. Although the pace is slower (see cover) there is no shortage of challenges, opportunities, sources of amazement and hilarious situations that beckon to us daily. A large number of the incidents worth reporting are related to one's own aging, but a substantial part of this book will be devoted to the observation of droll happenings that befall only older people.

This book's cover tells it all. The pace of a Geezer slows considerably. My rate is now down to 2.5 miles per hour.

I hope you enjoy this account of my life as a Geezer.

LIFE AS A GEEZER

LIFE AS A GEEZER

Chapter 1

A PAPER BLIZZARD

Although we Geezers don't retain the physical dexterity of our youth, we usually cope all right. When we fail, it's often because of bad luck. Several separate circumstances combine to force us into malfunction.

Such was the case with Richard's papers. Richard Lyon is the foreman at my onion-packing warehouse. He's also part owner and is the driving force behind the success of that operation.

I hired Richard when he was 23, some 35 years ago. He's still pretty young, but he has elected not to join the electronic age. He keeps our records in his own handwriting, meticulously entering each onion purchase or sale in all its complexity.

Richard is naturally a neat freak when it comes to his journals. There is never a doubt about which numeral or letter you are looking at when you examine the records. This is the exact opposite of my own handwriting efforts which resemble an unbreakable Sanskrit code.

But I'm still the guy who combines the records, files the tax returns and figures out our financial projections for the bank.

Thus it came to pass that I asked Richard for his growers' sales and settlement sheets so that I could compile a comprehensive financial review of our onion-packing year.

With painful memories from the past, Richard was reluctant to entrust me with his records. But, in deference to my age, he finally agreed. I placed the precious documents (200 pages) in my car, along with my dog and brief case, and made the two-mile trip from the packing shed to my office.

My dog, Nessie (the Loch Ness monster), cannot be trusted off her leash. This is especially true when entering my office as there is a 3-legged cat next door and she foolishly thinks she can catch it.

As I firmly believe in Dagwood Bumstead's "carry it all in one load" theory, I hooked up Nessie's leash, grabbed my brief case in one hand and Richard's papers in the other, and departed my vehicle.

I have this wonderful old Australian cowboy hat, a little too small, without which I feel naked. The hat was perched loosely on top of my head.

Nessie took off after the cat. The leash wrapped around me. My hat flew off. I grabbed for it and Richard's papers went flying. There was a stiff breeze and all the grower's sheets and manila folders blew across the road. There were numerous puddles from a recent rain and they were thick with Wilder mud that came from the beet trucks traveling to and from the receiving station across the street. Naturally the papers sought out the nearest puddles.

A sense of panic and dread overwhelmed me. How would I approach Richard and what would I tell him? Before I could formulate an answer, he came driving up. We gathered the papers in silence and placed them on the rug in my office so that they could dry.

But I knew that a soiled grower's sheet would not do for Richard. He would copy each jot and tittle in an exact duplicate of pounds of onions and pennies per bag even if it took him weeks to do it.

Richard is a fine fellow and he didn't give me a hard time. I had been proposing for a couple of years that we computerize our operation. He had stoutly resisted. But now he knew I was mortified and he wanted to make his elderly boss feel good.

"If we only had it on that computer we're going to buy, we'd just poke a button and the same records would come out again," he said.

We got the computer. Richard still won't use it. But, what the heck, I'm not really in sync with the electronic age either.

I caused Richard's papers to get wet.

Everything about Nessie
My name is Nessie (the Loch Ness Monster). I have a famous relative, Toto, star of the Wizard of Oz.

I am the arch-enemy of cats and they are terrified of me.

I don't miss many meals, so I have a pleasing waistline. I chase squirrels, ducks, rabbits, quail and any other varmints, but I love all dogs and all people, I visit nursing homes and let the old folks fawn over me.

My favorite toy
I love my little weasel. It's a nasty little brown toy that keeps me in shape for the real thing. Boy, I hate weasels.

My favorite foods
Anything fattening tossed from the dinner table. It's work, you know, to keep a respectable waistline.

Chapter 2

A TOUGH JOB

She came quietly carrying her poor aged pooch into the veterinary clinic. Her dog was wrapped tightly into an old blanket that had no doubt been his home base and source of comfort. I'll call the lady Sally and the dog Spot.

Spot wasn't a pretty dog with his short, motley-colored fur, receding jaw and pointed snout. But, oh those beautiful limpid eyes. You could look into his inner soul, and it was easy to see that his whole body was hurting. Dog and Mistress sat apart from us on the opposite side of the large waiting room.

My irrepressible cairn terrier, Nessie, was at the vet for a routine matter. She ran over to strike up an acquaintance, as was her wont with all dogs and all people. Sally did not object and managed a faint smile.

"It looks like your dog's not feeling well," I awkwardly offered, as I pulled Nessie away.

"I think it's his time," she said. I took a closer look and concluded there was no doubt about it. He was in miserable condition and certainly ready to go to that big doggie playground in the sky. I said, "It's one of the toughest jobs of all, parting with your dog." My mind flashed back to the final hour of

Nessie's predecessor. Sniffer, who served as First Dog of Idaho, had reached the age of sixteen. He went into serious decline, his poor mongrel body wracked by spasmodic coughing whenever he moved. Jacque wouldn't give up on him for a long time. But, finally, we decided he should suffer no more.

Jacque held him on her lap for most of the day, while I went to work. I took off from the governor's office early and removed him from her arms. The vet's clinic was less than a mile away. Sniffer licked my hand as we made the trip. It all went so fast. I handed him over to the assistant. Five minutes later the doctor gave me a plastic bag with poor dead Sniffer inside. I drove directly to my farm, 40 miles away, where the digging is easy, and placed him in with our previous cats and dogs and my famous mynah bird, Woodstock.

I snapped out of my reverie just as the nurse came out and said to Sally, "Bring him on in now." She quickly stood and made a firm path to the door of the operating room. She was doing her duty, but I noticed a tear rolling down her cheek. "Goodbye, Spot."

Chapter 3

SWEET JUSTICE

The Lord moves in mysterious ways – and sometimes it seems as if He needs to intervene more often.

I'm thinking of the multitude of problems caused by just plain rude drivers. Of course, reckless driving is a more serious matter because it causes more accidents. But hundreds of people each day are plunged into a foul mood just because of some uncaring clod behind the wheel of a motor vehicle.

I'm not the best driver myself and I've endured more than a few honkings, some well-deserved and some not. But I try to keep my impatience under control, to let people come into my lane and to be reasonably thoughtful.

Not so for too many others. It seems for some that to show any deference to other motorists is a fatal character flaw.

But sometimes crass behavior doesn't pay. Jacque and I were tooling along on a major artery in Boise. Traffic was heavy and nearly everyone was resigned to waiting through a couple of cycles at the traffic lights.

A very large 4-wheel drive vehicle appeared in my rear-view mirror. That pickup was the size of a small tank with wheels that looked like they were borrowed from heavy construction equipment. The driver wanted to get in the left-turn lane and he was in no mood to wait. There was a large island about 12 inches high and extending a long way back. The tank driver would have to wait a while for the lane entry to become available.

No problem, he decided, and he went up over the island settling comfortably in the left-turn lane only a couple of lengths from the light.

What he had failed to notice was that a cop's car was now directly on his right. I expect that the policeman chuckled a little at this easy catch. One toot on the siren and Mr. Gargantuan Rude was pulled over. He probably got a pretty good jolt in traffic court. It was richly deserved.

Chapter 4

THE GOLDEN AGE

The Golden Age may be golden all right, but it's certainly not steel. All of the Geezer's faculties become impaired.

Eyesight and hearing are most heavily impacted. But, touch and taste and smell aren't what they used to be either.

I lived on the farm all my life until I came to Boise for gubernatorial service. In the country we don't worry much about doggie doo. Fido usually goes in some unseen place, and even when it's on your own lawn, it's not that big of a deal.

Not so in the city. The pet often decides to make a deposit during walk time. Two walks a day can result in two piles in plain sight of the public. So, Jacque and I are well-prepared to clean up the mess.

There is a wonderful invention called the mutt mitt. It is a white plastic bag with a black plastic insert sealed in the bottom. When doggie does his thing, you reach through the open top, grab the prize with the black insert, and then invert and envelop the black part with the white. No muss, no fuss! Nothing on the hands, nothing in sight. It's such a good seal that there's usually not that much odor. I stick the finished product in my coat pocket while I complete the walk.

Don't forget to remove the doggy-doo sack from the Holiday Packing Co. coat.

I'm getting better about hanging up my coat in my old age. I have these two identical Holiday Packing Company coats. They came from my onion shed and they are ideal for dog walking. They sometimes have their own onion odor which fills me with pleasant nostalgia.

Jacque's nose is better than mine. One day she informed me that there was a foul smell coming out of my closet.

Upon inspection, I found a mutt mitt in one of my coats that I had not discarded after use. Time had ripened it and the offending bag was quickly disposed of.

That restored calm to the household for a day. But I then was informed that air quality in the Batt domicile was still not ideal. Yes, the second Holiday Packing coat's pockets yielded the same obnoxious contents.

Now, I have altered my routine. The first thing I do after doggie's walk is to empty my pockets. Only then do I remove her leash.

Who says an old Geezer can't learn new tricks?

Chapter 5

SUCH LOVE

Southwest Airlines is my favorite. It's a bit of an aggravation to stand in line an hour early in order to get a good seat. But they have the loading scenario down to a science. The seats are comfortable. The crew is energetic and attentive. Best of all, Southwest departs and arrives on time.

Most of their airplanes are divided by a bulkhead between fore and aft. At the seam are 6 seats facing rearward. There is ample seat space in the bulkhead, which compensates for having to look other passengers in the eye.

I was a couple of rows back from the rearward-facing seats on a recent leg from Oakland to Reno. A family occupied the bulkhead seats that were exposed to my view.

They appeared to be of Italian descent. Father, probably 50 years old, sat by the window. Mother, a couple of years younger, took the aisle. In the center was a radiant young lady. It wasn't hard to figure out that she was about to become a bride.

She was an effervescent maiden, with an expressive face that regularly gave off a quick smile. She wore a black and white baseball cap and a matching sweatshirt. Her good looks were natural, with no attempt to reach the status of a raving beauty.

Upon her lap, protected by an open box, was the bridal bouquet. It was a masterpiece of large and small white flowers, set off by a bit of green. She held it with a firm grip. Nobody was going to make off with it.

While there was no doubt about their happiness, a small amount of apprehension resided in each of them. They were so close to each other. There was such family love.

Father stared out the window. It was his job to be the family comedian. At sporadic intervals he would point out something on the horizon or in the airplane. He'd make a humorous observation and they'd all convulse into laughter.

Then reality would take over and the young lady would entwine her arms with both parents, still clutching her bouquet. With sober faces, they'd savor the moment. Such love.

Mother seemed the most at ease. She would periodically put her arm around the prospective bride and kept up a running conversation about everything and nothing.

But it was easy to tell that her thoughts, and each of their thoughts, were on how their lives would be changed, how this close-knit trio would be required to subordinate itself to someone new.

Would the bride's new union be as happy as the old one with her family? It seemed improbable. Yet, history is on the side of the newlyweds, and with the wondrous love present among

14

them, I'm betting that the lucky groom will have a great marriage.

The airplane came to a halt at the gate, and the bride clutched her bouquet even tighter. I wondered how they liked my probing eyes. Not to worry. As I passed by, I whispered, "Good luck!" Each of the three gave me a million-dollar smile.

Such family solidarity took me back in time to a certain winter day in 1948.

Jacque and I had just eloped and married and we traversed the long country road to the power generating station on the Spokane River managed by her father. This was how they were to learn that their only daughter was a married woman.

We burst in at the door and our radiant faces gave us away. "Are you engaged? Are you married?" they asked in quick succession. "Yes! Yes!" And they quickly embraced us both. Such love!

Chapter 6

_____

WORKING AT THE CAR WASH

I was in the public eye for a long time and, consequently, a lot of people recognize me. Most of the time that's a good thing as the encounters are almost always pleasant.

Yet it takes a good dose of reality at times to emphasize that fame is, indeed, fleeting.

My regular barber was out of town and I was in dire need of a haircut. I decided to hunt up the closest tonsorial establishment and take my chances. So what if I'd get a white sidewall job? Who cares at my age?

I found a place called "Great Clips" only a few blocks away and walked in.

A young woman named Jody greeted me. She looked to be about 25 and, with her miniskirt and long curly hair, she was quite attractive. "There's one ahead of you," she said.

Being Mr. Impatient, I asked how long that would be. I suggested a half-hour. "Oh, no," said Jody, "about five minutes."

I settled in and seven minutes later, as I was just getting to the interesting part of the magazine, she announced that it was my turn.

A quick dose of the water spritz bottle and she was snipping away.

There was little time for small talk, she mostly asked about the height of my sideburns and the hair that sprouts off my ears, like thistles, in my old age.

It was obvious that she didn't know me from Adam. She had taken my name, however, and she suddenly asked, "Do you have a son?" "Yes, Ma'am," I replied, "he's a lawyer here in town." "Well, doesn't he play keyboards?" she countered.

Bill Batt, attorney by day and rock musician by night, with his mother, Jacque.

My son, Bill, sometimes works all day at lawyering and then plays rock music until 2 a.m. I seldom hear him 'cause that's way past my bedtime. I told Jody all that and she said, "Well, he's really good."

I agreed, but my time was up. In less than five minutes I had received a 'great clip.' Pretty dang good cut, too, at half the price I've been paying.

But, back to that short period of time when I was waiting my turn. A lady came in with her three small children, all of whom would soon have their five minutes in the chair.

She looked at me quizzically and I said hello. She kept taking a glance and you could tell that she was trying to remember where she'd seen me.

To put her at ease, I offered, "Mighty good-looking kids." That did it. She felt as if she'd have to find out who I was. "Thanks," she said. And then, "Say, don't you work at that car wash down the street?" "No," I replied. "I've done a lot of things, including being your Governor, but I never worked in a car wash."

"Well," she concluded, "you look like the gray-haired old guy who works there."

*   *   *   *

Car washes are often the scene of droll happenings. One day, when I was governor, my assistant Claudia took my car down to the wash. The young lady in charge was impressed by the license plate. "How do you get #1?" she asked. Claudia, who is never at a loss for a quick retort, replied, "You win it in the

19

lottery, my dear." "Gosh," said the girl, "I'm going to buy some tickets."

Chapter 7

SENIOR DISCOUNTS

Twenty years ago when I reached the ripe old age of 55, I received a notice informing me that I was eligible to join AARP, a "senior citizen"organization. It would cost only $5 annually and it promised numerous benefits, so I signed up. Soon I could receive discounts for a slew of expenditures, such as motels and restaurants.

At first I was reluctant to admit my age and passed up many a senior saving. But, in time, I became as greedy as the next person and took full advantage of all those reductions.

I soon dropped AARP because its lobbyists became so aggressive in demanding concessions from Congress. To hear their pitch, you'd think this generation of seniors is the only reason the USA has survived and prospered. The government should show its gratitude to its older folks of all income levels by fattening up Social Security checks and paying for everything from ingrown toenails to total health care to bad hair days to subsidized housing, according to AARP.

Never mind that the 60 and over age group has more income per capita than any other. Lobbyists for seniors never give an inch. When some members of Congress proposed that a higher premium be paid for Medicare by those who could afford it, a howl of protest killed the idea. Let Bill Gates collect government largesse too, they demanded, even if the trust funds are headed for insolvency.

But I digress. Private retail establishments give discounts for a purpose, generally to attract more customers. If seasoned citizens get a price break, they'll come to the restaurant more often and so will their kids and grandkids. After all, kids and oldsters alike have a great time remembering when little Susie put the mashed potatoes on Grandpa's bald head.

Among the most universal of senior discounts are those offered at the movies and I'm a bit puzzled by this. We all know the owners make their big money by selling 8 ounces of popcorn for $5. But seniors have a hard time with popcorn because of their dentures. Also, none of them can sit through a 2-hour movie, after downing a 32-ounce Coke, without groping in the dark in search of a bathroom.

No doubt the cinematic entrepreneurs think it pays to give the oldsters a break at the ticket office. Yet the age of the average moviegoer continues to decline.

I have a suggestion for the movie moguls if they really want more of us old folks to come in. Limit the content of the movies as follows:
  1. No more than three killings per half-hour.
  2. A maximum of 10 times of the use of the word f—-'———-n per movie.
  3. Please hide the orgasms behind a curtain for the 'G' rated movies.

Chapter 8

VACUUMING BY A MATURE PERSON

Those of you who have read my previous book know that I was possessed by mowermania for several decades. I used to mow the lawns of all my family members and friends and sometimes of perfect strangers.

I don't have a pickup to haul my mower anymore and I don't have the strength required for all that exertion. Those days have gone, along with other youthful foolishness. Yet, certain mundane chores still hold a fascination for me.

Most prominent among those is vacuuming. It's not that I am really fond of that assignment. But, with all the skills and tricks of the trade that I have acquired, it would be a real waste not to employ them.

I hereby impart some of the knowledge I have gleaned over many years of vacuuming.

First, regard the electric cord as the implacable enemy. The person who invents a full-fledged cordless vacuum (a prototype is the Dustbuster) will have struck a gold mine.

The cord has an uncanny way of getting in front of you. As I have grown older and wiser, I keep excess cordage coiled in my hand.

Even so, the cord will wrap around the vacuum and tangle with your feet when you least expect it.

Don't succumb to the temptation to see how far the cord will reach. A 20-foot cord will always pull out of the wall socket at 15 feet if you have only a small corner to go.

Do not fail to allow 6 inches more leeway than you think is necessary when directing the vacuum around the furniture and wall corners. Otherwise, the machine will lunge at furniture and walls, leaving black marks, and arousing the ire of the chief household engineer (your spouse). If you want to make a big hit with the boss, actually move the furniture and put it back after the carpet is cleaned. It takes 15 minutes longer – time well spent in return for a tranquil household.

I don't care if my vacuum can lift an 8-pound bowling ball, but I do want to be able to rescue it when it is trapped. The power drive on the new models is nice, but it often causes the vacuum to dive for that corner between the end table and the sofa. It has no reverse and so must be picked directly up for removal.

Vacuum cleaner manufacturers have a secret pact which will not allow any of them to install a top handle. Therefore, lifting a machine out of entrapment causes a lot of sweating and cursing. And, when you finally succeed, you find that the cord has been eaten by the vacuum, pulling it from the wall socket and blowing a fuse.

It is highly frustrating when the bag is full and you have no replacements left. But don't fake it – running the machine over the rug with a full bag merely spreads it around. Go down to the store and buy some new bags. In the case of my old Panasonic, this means you must go to a store specializing in such rare antique items. When you vacuum on Sunday or after hours, the store will be closed. No problem. Take the old bag outside, where flying dust doesn't matter, and carefully pull the wads of lint through the tiny hole. It will only take one hour and if you haven't poked a hole in the old bag, you're back in business.

Do not make the mistake of thinking that you can vacuum up against chairs where shoelaces, apron strings or brassiere straps are hanging down. These appendages will leap at a vacuum, multiplying their length several times and bringing the machine to a halt while filling the air with the smell of burning rubber.

I feel better now that I have unburdened myself of these valuable observations. Further, I must attest that when the job is done, one can look out upon the vast expanse of dirt-free carpet with satisfaction.

Man has once again mastered the machine.

Chapter 9

LINE CRASHERS

Green Valley, Arizona is great in the wintertime: comfortable daytime temperatures; beautiful surroundings; abundant, affordable golf courses; hiking trails and other recreational facilities.

The biggest bonus of all is the retirees themselves. They come from all over, but mainly from the northern climes. Michigan, Minnesota and other areas with nasty winter weather are heavily represented.

Most of these people have been reasonably successful and are now reaping the benefits of good planning toward retirement.

I like to go out on the golf course as a single, and listen to the life stories of those who were perfect strangers until the golf starter matched us up.

They are college professors, engineers, company executives and salesmen, CPAs, lawyers, investment entrepreneurs, retail clerks, and a thousand other trades. They've belonged to all kinds of service groups and fraternal organizations. With few exceptions, they are unfailingly polite. They're proud of their families and of their careers, and they're genuinely interested in yours. (I don't tell them about my political activities, unless I'm forced into it.)

On the golf course, Green Valleyans go out of their way to keep from offending anyone. And it's the same with most other activities in that fair village. But there are two glaring exceptions. One is the pervasive road rage, which I'll elaborate on later. The other is the uncivilized behavior that reverberates through the Safeway grocery store and parking lot.

Safeway has a good store in Green Valley and it is a gold mine for the chain. Most of the populated area is centered around the store and thus it has kind of a captive clientele. It is usually overcrowded with shoppers, except in the evening. Green Valley residents ordinarily hit the sack about 7 p.m.

Good parking lot spots are at a premium during peak hours at Safeway. The old duffers think nothing of holding up traffic for 15-20 minutes if they think a choice spot will soon be vacant. But, it's worse inside.

Thrusting that many people together generates a lot of ill will. Nobody likes to spend grocery money in the first place, and the crowded aisles don't offer much in the way of personal space. It's not uncommon to see one lady snatch up an item just as another has laid hands on it.

The worst bickering occurs at the checkout line. Safeway probably thought it had enough checkout space when the store was built. But now pandemonium reigns. The lines are forced to blend and carts clash with each other. Some patrons purposely ram others. With the confusion in lines many opportunists try to ace out someone ahead of them.

One shopper grew so angry that he threw potatoes at the hapless clerk. Another time, two old goats got in a fistfight and the police had to be called. Another one flipped his lid and went running through the store, shouting that he was going to die.

But the number of these male outbursts pales in comparison to those on the distaff side. Ordinarily genteel ladies turn into rude savages. Dirty looks and cart bumping abound.

It's not a happy scene and the ill humor is infectious. Even those good-natured Safeway employees sometimes turn pugnacious.

I've taken to evening grocery shopping. All is well then, and I can look forward to a lot of polite people on the golf course the next day.

Chapter 10

LOOKIN' GOOD

"When I was young I had lots of pep, used to get around; did-n't need no he'p. But now that I'm a gettin' old and gray people just look at me and say: He's gettin' too old – he's done got too old. He's too old to cut the mustard anymore."

I'm so old that I can remember when the Dead Sea was just getting sick. I don't really care. Aging is a natural process so I don't deserve any credit or any blame for this chain of events.

I reveled in being young, and have also been pleased with all the stages of my life. I'd reverse some of the mistakes I've made if I had the chance, but by and large each year brings new adventures and new perspectives.

Senior years have been referred to as the "Golden Age." That's a good nomenclature, but the gold (as Omar Khayyam reminded us) is sometimes "dross-allay'd." The ability to reflect on events of the past with neutral judgment is never as keen as in old age. It's a relief to review one's lifespan with a minimum of prejudice and a large dose of realism. Yet, the physical infirmities of an aging body are bothersome and, in too many cases, debilitating and devastating.

Lookin' good in the desert.

Some oldsters yearn to go back and start over – not I. It would rob the later years of any meaning.

Thus, I'm amused when I meet up with people I haven't seen for awhile. Inevitably, one of us will say, "You're sure looking good," or, "You don't look any older." The person saying this really means it but it must be taken in context. Each expects to see something worse.

Why, I don't know. Aging is a gradual process and even over a year's time there is usually not any radical change in a person's appearance. That's not to say we don't look different as we grow older. But, unless you're dead, people shouldn't expect you to look like a cadaver.

I'm just thankful people care enough to assess my appearance. And, if they say, "You're sure looking good," I'm pleased as punch.

Chapter 11

PUTTIN' ON THE TUX, WITHOUT JACQUE

I'm not much of a fan of tuxedos and I've managed to avoid wearing one except on rare occasions. However, I do get stuck now and then. In fact, I bought one when I became Governor of Idaho.

It's not that I don't think they're handsome. If you like the sight of dozens of penguins conversing with each other (and I do) you can appreciate tuxedos.

Furthermore tuxedos, with their uniformity, tend to obscure the lack of handsomeness that bedevils many of us. Mr. Hunk looks almost like Mr. Milquetoast when they are both wearing tuxes.

Well, I bought one. But with my lack of experience, I naturally ended up with shirt studs that were too small. It made the insertion of the studs slightly easier, but they offered only a tenuous connection to the shirt. My pot-bellied build, when I sat down, would sometimes release the button stud. This was especially embarrassing when I looked down at my napkin during a White House dinner and saw a large expanse of my skin appearing where the stud had come loose.

That hard lesson caused me to buy another set of hardware and things have been going along quite smoothly. When I have to don the tux, Jacque helps me through the tortuous process. The studs hold, and everyone says I look great.

But fate played a cruel trick on me recently. It became necessary to wear the tux and I had to assemble it on my own.

The occasion was the Gene Harris Jazz Festival. My late friend Gene Harris, one of the all-time champion performers of jazz music, originated a music festival at Boise State University. As I am a musical curiosity, he asked me to sit in with my clarinet for a couple of numbers. This went on annually until Gene's untimely death in 2000. The Festival still carries on in his memory and I have been honored to perform each of several years.

The first time I played, I asked Gene if I'd have to wear my tux. "Yes," he replied, "you may not sound good, but you'll look good!"

That was fine until last year. When the time rolled around, Jacque was out of town. As I had been totally dependent upon her to dress me, I was on the alert for trouble. I made elaborate preparations. All clothes were freshly cleaned; shoes shined; inventory of accessories complete.

How long should I allow for dressing after showering – a half-hour? Not enough, make it one hour. Everything was laid out in a neat line - one, two, three, go!

On with the shirt. The larger studs may hold good but they are devilishly hard to insert. I'd clipped my fingernails (the better to play the clarinet) and it was really slow going. The sleeve studs were relatively easy. No more than 3 minutes each even though they go through 4 layers.

Now to the front shirt studs. The bottom two went in fairly well, then the next up. It resisted, but I was up to the challenge – pop – in it went. Now for the biggie – the top one. Why is it so tough to tell what you're doing in a mirror? Move it farther in – no, farther out – more up, more down – left – right. Sweating and cursing, jumping up and down on one foot or the other, I finally triumphed. A total of 18 minutes for the shirt hardware. Not bad, but no extra time for fooling around – continue with the process.

The bow tie is the work of the archfiend. If I could form the bow from a long piece of black cloth it would not be so bad, but I don't have the skill to fashion a bow tie so I have to rely on a pre-tied beauty that snaps around the neck. You hook the snap in front and then move the tie around. It has to be extremely tight or it will sag and destroy the penguin image. Try as I might, I could not get the tiny hook into the tinier clasp. I tried it with the mirror for awhile, then without the mirror, hoping I could sneak up on it. My fingers were going numb from exerting useless pressure on the non-hook area.

I gave up and decided I'd have to leave it hanging until I got assistance at the event. But, just as King Bruce of Scotland decided to give it one last try, I fiercely lunged at it again. Miracle of miracles, the tie snapped into place. A half-hour had now elapsed.

The suspender hooking to the pants was rather routine. The toughest choice was deciding which side of the galluses goes

Gene Harris said, "Wear your tux!"

out. Put the shiny black part outside, Dummy, I told myself. Yes, that was much better than showing the brown rawhide. The pants were on! Thirty-eight minutes down.

Now for the most sensible part of the outfit – the cummerbund. This piece of pleated cloth covers all, including pot-bellies. If only they designed it so it would go clear up to the Adam's apple they could save a hell of a lot of trouble.

But, which way do the pleats go – up or down? I remembered what General Darrell Manning once told me: "Catch the soup, the pleats go up."

The coat and shoes offered no resistance and I was ready. It only took a cool 40 minutes. Why did I set aside a whole hour?

Chapter 12

BEAUTY CAN BE REPELLING

We Geezers take only a mild interest in beauty pageants. When we were young we would really give the models the eyeball if we thought our wives weren't watching, which they always were out of the corners of their eyes. Now we genuinely yawn instead of faking it.

I usually read most of the newspaper. If I leave any out it's the Life Section. That's where various and sundry events are reported that are of little interest to men.

But it was a slow day so I thumbed through the Life Section. What's this? A report on a young lady who had just won the right to represent our state in the Miss America Pageant. I'll read on.

The accompanying pictures left no doubt that she climbed rocks for a pastime. Well, to each his or her own. I sometimes have rocks in my head but have never had the desire to scale up treacherous inclines and maim or kill myself.

Why would she choose such divertissement? The article said it's because she likes repelling - a strange desire for a person whose success depends on people liking her.

Could she mean rappelling, an action common among rock climbers? I scanned the entire feature.

No, it was repelling, repeated several times throughout the article. Now, let's reason this out. She would not want to repel the judges or the audience itself at beauty pageants. Therefore, it must have something to do with mountain climbing or the outdoors in general. Maybe she has developed a new karma that repels rocks and makes them afraid of her.

Or maybe it's not rocks at all. Mosquitoes are ubiquitous in the outdoors and perhaps she just wants to repel them.

In any case, I'm proud of her and wish her great success. I'm sure she'll win the talent section because she's likely the only contestant in her unique field of repelling.

Chapter 13

MEXICAN AND CHINESE CUISINE

I was born outside of Wilder, Idaho and lived there for some 65 years. I watched as it grew from a pioneer outpost to a thriving farm village and then I still watched as it receded into almost total economic decay.

At one time, Wilder boasted about 35 retail establishments. Now there are only a handful and most of the one-time flourishing shops have been boarded up or torn down. Wilder's retail trade met the fate of most small towns. Bigger and better and cheaper retailers have made it impossible for the tiny shops of the past to survive. The trend continues as giants such as Wal-Mart and Home Depot swallow up medium-sized stores that looked secure only a few years ago.

Where will it end? Who knows? Maybe electronic shopping will replace the whole scene. The ingenuity of American entrepreneurs is unlimited and I'm proud of our free-enterprise system. But, it hurts my head to think about it. So, back to Wilder.

Every town, unless it has gasped its last breath, has a café. And Wilder has always had one - not the same one, of course. Some café owners have handed it down to their children, some have died off, some have retired and some have gone broke. But, by hook or by crook, Wilder has always had a café. Except for two times. One of those harrowing episodes occurred about 15 years ago, when the last in a string of owners threw up his hands.

A certain second cousin of mine got the idea that this failure occurred for lack of a spacious, modern facility. As he is related to me he is naturally a tightwad, so he decided that everyone should participate in the pain. He formed a small corporation and sold stock in a proposed new café.

Nobody in Wilder wants to be cheaper than the rest of the cheapskates, so we all bought stock and a new modern café emerged from the dust. The entirely predictable fact that our investment would become worthless did not dampen our pride at the grand opening.

Life was good and we could order up homemade cinnamon rolls. Some wag labeled them "death wads" because he said they'd swell up inside of you and kill you. The name stuck and each new operator prided himself or herself on the quality of these gastronomical curiosities.

Well, the same building, The Furrow Cafe, still stands today. It has gone through several lessees/owners and, unfortunately, the last one called it quits a couple of years ago.

That resulted in the second time Wilder has been without a café, an intolerable situation. However, a new savior has come to the rescue. It was breathlessly announced that the restaurant would open again with Hispanic food.

Excellent! Si bueno! The sign on the soon-to-open establishment read: "Opening Soon – Mexican Cuisine."

This is the first time Wilderites have been treated to cuisine of any kind. It was a little confusing, so one of the locals asked my onion shed foreman, "Have you seen the new restaurant? They're going to serve Mexican and Chinese."

Well, Mexican anyway.

Late Bulletin: The café has closed – exotic menu and all! Maybe we can get one of Boise's excess hot dog vendors to open up a stand in Wilder.

Chapter 14

SHOOTING ONE'S AGE AT GOLF

I am usually bashful about putting my fantasies on display to be pooh-poohed by the cynical public. But I now confess that I am obsessed by the thought of shooting my age at golf.

I am a hacker and I carry a 21 handicap. I'm halfway through my 70s and I've never come close to scoring that well and no doubt never will, but I can dream. Can't I?

When I am wintering in Green Valley, Arizona, I play with a wide variety of geezers. Many are older than I – some into their nineties.

I've seen some really good golfers out there. I played once with an 86-year-old who shot 84. It can be done. But the infirmities of old age relentlessly tend to cancel out the advantage of lowering the target score.

Those old guys are tough. I played with one 82-year-old who would take a swat at the ball and then lie down in his cart and take a few puffs on his oxygen bottle before resuming play. Another had his back go out on the first hole. He flopped down on the ground and performed his knee bends. That worked for a while but he gave up before he reached the third green.

But the average of the retirees there is in pretty good shape. They can't see or hear very well but they take a mighty cut at the pellet and the results are pretty good. I've seen two of them shoot their age and several more say they've done it.

So, back to assessing my chances. The best I've ever scored is an 84, when I was 75 years old. That's only 9 strokes off. Now let's look at Tiger Woods. He's 26 years old and has probably never shot less than 56. He's 30 strokes off! He does have a lot of distractions such as signing autographs and collecting enormous checks.

I once bowled 200 and know that I'd never reach 300. I don't care. I've broken 25 clay pigeons in a row with my shotgun. Yet, I'm certain that I could never pulverize a string of 50, let alone 100. I'm resigned to it. It causes me no angst. But the dream harbored by Philip Mitty Batt of shooting his age at golf lives on.

Technology is my friend. Breakthroughs in golf club design occur regularly and the new golf balls lengthen each drive 10 or 20 yards even for duffers. Price is no object. So what if I have to mortgage my house and my dog to buy another set of new clubs. Bring on the golf lessons. Bring on long hours on the course and the driving range. I am a man possessed.

And, some fine summer day in 2009, when I'm 82 years old, carrying a new plutonium-coated driver and a spring-loaded putter and playing on the 67 par Caldwell Municipal Golf Course, I will post the incredible score of 82.

Pocketa, pocketa, pocketa.

Governor Andrus, Jim Yost, Rich Cortez, and me in our new golf outfits.

Chapter 15

PLAYING BUMPER CARS FOR REAL

Driving can be hazardous at any age. Young, bold drivers have the worst accident rate. So we opportunistic seasoned citizens use that argument when there is any attempt to circumscribe our driving freedom.

This was the prevailing excuse when the Arizona Legislature killed a proposed law for testing aged drivers. It called for a mandatory eye test when a person over 70 years old had received two tickets for driving infractions over a year's period.

The measure was unceremoniously dumped in committee. That action spoke volumes about the importance of the senior snowbirds who fuel a billion-dollar portion of Arizona's economy.

A lot of Green Valley drivers never go fast enough to inflict serious injury (see cover) but they do cause many harrowing moments. One bumper sticker sums it up: "Helen Keller is alive and well and driving in Green Valley."

The automobile of choice is the Lincoln Town Car, which is big and boxy and heavy – the better to cream the hapless compacts.

Fender benders are common. News reports of such events only bring out yawns but, other notable events happen too. A 91-year-old woman recently drove through a show window and ended up entirely within the establishment. That's drive-in shopping for you.

Another oldster was arrested on the freeway a couple of miles outside of town for driving his golf cart while intoxicated. What he was doing out there past curfew remains a mystery as he could not explain it.

Golf carts are ubiquitous in Green Valley. Their drivers like to think they own the road. I guess they do. After all, they pay taxes. There are special lanes set aside for them. Thank Goodness! Because the flimsy machines are no match for a Lincoln Town Car. More times than can be justified the cart drivers leave the lanes and take their chances in traffic. Those drivers are usually non-golfers who use golf carts as their sole means of transportation.

There seems to be a rule among senior automobile drivers that you should never let another car into your lane. Thus, like Charlie on the MTA, someone out for an errand may never return because he couldn't change lanes in order to turn off at his designation.

There are so many disabled drivers that a large percentage of parking places are reserved for those who suffer from limited physical ability. That's not so bad. But what gets to me is that some drivers will use 2 or 3 parking spaces when they cruise up to a store.

Inevitably, vigorous protests arise from one driver to another. There is usually no shouting and the display of the middle finger is quite rare. The weapon of choice is the car horn and its blare fills the air with great regularity. But not after 9 p.m. All Green Valleyans are in bed by that time.

There are hundreds of golf carts.

Chapter 16

GEEZARAS

It is not hard to find plenty of epithets to describe old men, dirty or not. We are old devils or codgers or coots. But no label is quite as useful as "Geezers."

"Geezers" is not exactly complimentary, but neither is it pejorative. It is non-judgmental. It merely describes a class of oldsters.

The thought occurs to me that no such comparable term applies to the female of the species. There are plenty of attempts to describe older women but they tend to unduly flatter or to malign them.

Many an older man lovingly refers to his wife as "The Little Woman." But you can't describe all of them that way. What about the ones who are two ax-handles wide? You can't call them "The Big Woman" either unless you want to get in a lot of trouble.

So, I have dedicated myself to finding a proper title for the multitude of older women. Such a classification is needed since there are many more of them than older men because of their remarkable and superior longevity.

Men are prone to call each other "Old Farts." It is a semi-endearing term. I saw a couple the other day. The man was wearing a T-shirt identifying him as "Old Fart." His wife was wearing one that was labeled "Old Fart's Wife." Now wait a minute. Let's have a little equality here. What would NOW have to say about this? I'll bet if you called Pat Schroeder an "Old Fart's Wife" she'd deck you with a right hook.

No, we must look further. Crones and battleaxes are out. Men get in enough hot water by using those terms.

How about "Geezerettes?" It has a nice ring to it but the same problem exists. It sounds as if the women are only auxiliary to the men.

It must be something of equal status such as "women" is to "men." I've got it – "Geezaras." That's every bit as authoritative and mellifluous as "Geezers."

But, please, no national organizations. The national association of Geezaras would always be known as NAG. Stay independent, so that hubby can lovingly refer to you as his own private Geezara. Maybe he'll even build you a gazebo.

Chapter 17

CELL PHONES

There's a fierce debate going on about the safety of driving while talking on a cell phone. Talk shows are engrossed with the argument and proponents and opponents alike seem unwilling to give an inch.

No doubt gabbing to a remote person while handling a 2-ton pile of steel is not a good thing, but neither are a long list of other activities routinely carried out by drivers while traversing our highways and byways.

I'll have to come down on the side of freedom and oppose mandatory hang-up laws. But I recognize the danger. In fact, I have almost stopped the practice myself. I generally use my mobile phone only when I'm parked.

This is not to say I don't engage in questionable practices. The worst is playing hand-wrestling games with my little dog while tooling along. She usually starts it but sometimes – well, it gets a little boring and I give her a shove and away we go.

Yet, I don't engage in some of the other distractions. Lots of ladies apply lipstick or comb their hair while driving. I don't use lipstick and my hair is so sparse that I can comb it in 10 seconds at my destination.

I don't read newspapers while at the wheel. At least I haven't since I was about 30 years old and scared hell out of myself when I almost ran into a ditch out by Wilder.

The other day, I saw a motorist brushing his teeth while driving. He was using a battery-powered toothbrush, which was probably safer than a manual one. He was concentrating pretty hard on his toothbrushing. It would really be distracting if he rolled down the window to spit.

Fiddling with the radio also ruins one's driving concentration. It's not worth it. The next station will be just as bad as the one you just left. Leave it alone. Strap your kids in and ignore them until you get where you're going. A good set of earplugs will help you through the ordeal.

But, back to cell phones. Why is it that people bellow into them? You wouldn't let a stranger listen in on your phone conversation at home, but it seems as if the mobile phone user wants everyone to hear.

I've seen them in hotels or stores detailing every facet of their personal lives for all and sundry to hear. There's no shame. They'll ask the neighbor's wife, in a loud tone, if hubby is not home so they can share a little afternoon delight.

It's almost as if they think no one can hear them. It's kind of like when you go in a bar and have a couple of blasts. You get thinking you are invisible and you can make a perfect fool of yourself without being detected.

Unfortunately, it's not so in either case but loud mobile phoners don't care – they holler away. I have a solution for those with leather lungs – let them just roll down the car window and shout. It would be safer than using a phone and they could be heard all the way from Boise to Mountain Home.

Chapter 18

WITH A SONG IN MY HEART

When I was a kid I always had a song in my heart and, most of the time, on my lips too. I would whistle and sing a good share of the time clear up into adulthood.

But the voice falters and the whistle pucker becomes imperfect. In time my lips fell silent, but the song remained in my heart. Most days, even now, I wake with a song running through my head. It becomes maddening when the same one stays for many days in a row. And it's usually a tune that I didn't care for in its heyday.

For instance "Candy": "I call my Sugar Candy and it'll be just dandy, to make her mine, all mine." I hate that song and it parks in my head for a week at a time. It's far better when the Hallelujah Chorus from Handel's "Messiah" bursts forth in all its glory, but it can overstay its welcome also.

The jingle from Nu-Look Car Wash always seems pleasant no matter how long the stay. ("Nu-Look Car Wash; Nu-Look Car Wash, good as new.")

Sometimes the old timers appear – "What'll I Do" (the plaintive question trails off – "When you and I are through, what'll

I do, what'll I do, what'll I do?) It makes me want to comfort the poor soloist.

One of the most welcome returning songs is "Teddy Bears' Picnic." ("If you go out in the woods today, you're in for a big surprise—for today's the day the teddy bears have their picnic.") No matter how many days the bears march through my brain, I'm delighted to have them.

Occasionally a wholly original tune will appear. This morning phenomenon is how I came to write "Freedom Idaho" and "Jacque Elaine Waltz." But I seldom burst into song. And the last time anyone asked me to sing was 30 or 40 years ago when we all got half-snockered and I led the Christmas carols.

However, I was playing my clarinet in a Dixieland Band at the baseball game a couple of months ago and someone thought it would be a novel idea for me to lead the crowd through a rendition of "Take Me Out to the Ballgame." So, during the seventh inning stretch, we trooped onto the field and I got my big moment. It was such a rousing success that I have now done it four or five times. Waving my clarinet wildly through the air, with eyes bulging, I shout, "It's one, two, three strikes you're out at the old ballgame."

I haven't been asked for any off-field performances and I don't expect any requests. I am secure, though, in the knowledge that my fixation with songs in my head has been passed on.

My granddaughter Anna, now sixteen, has not missed a day without a song in her head and she sings and whistles with gay abandon. May it continue forever.

Three fifths of the Capitol City Jazz Band.

Chapter 19

HI-TECH FOR A LOW-TECH SENIOR

I'm only half computer literate and not even that far into the information age in general. That's okay because you don't have to be a hi-tech whiz to be awestruck by these incredible advances.

I have this $29.95 watch. The band's a little tight so I hadn't worn it for a couple of years. I had an alternative watch given to me by Ed McMahon. He was in town promoting Nabisco products when I was Governor. His company had discovered that Boise, Idaho consumed, per capita, more Ritz crackers, saltines and other Nabisco products than any other city.

The Nabisco Company held contests in all 50 states, crowning, as state champions, the creator of the most ingenious display made of its products. There were some dandies – ships built of Triscuits, male and female dolls fabricated entirely from Ritz crackers doing intricate dances, etc.

The company brought all the state winners to Boise. Each arrived in a separate limousine at the Egyptian Theater. I emceed the event and the inimitable Ed McMahon made the whole affair hilarious.

He presented me with a "Ritz" watch for my efforts. I love the watch, but it finally gave up the ghost and the store told me I'd have to cough up $185 if I wished to extend its life.

That was too stiff for me. I removed my $29.95 Timex from the drawer. It had gained less than 3 minutes in two years.

I remember being covetous of my father's pocket watch when I was a kid. If I had been a good boy he'd hold it up to my ear and let me listen. But when he gave it the daily winding he also adjusted it two or three minutes. We are a lot better off watch-wise.

Perhaps more of a wonder are computerized traffic signals. These intricate devices can be set in a complex pattern to allow the flow of traffic with minimum delays. I have never heard of any accident being caused by a malfunctioning traffic light. Think of the liability that would accrue to the manufacturer and/or the Highway Department if crossing lanes got the green light at the same time. They're working even better than stop signs.

I resisted automatic teller machines long after they came available. Now I wouldn't think of bothering to get cash by any other means. Yet I have wondered – how can these devices operate so well that neither side gets cheated? I counted my money religiously at first. Then I decided they never make a mistake. That's almost true. The other day I was replenishing my wallet when, halfway through the process, the machine sputtered and stopped spewing out bills. But after a couple of seconds it resumed again. Then the robot gave me fair warning. "Possible error – count your cash," the message said. I did, and I was $20 short.

The bank made it good, but the miracle was that the machine was smart enough to know that it might be wrong. That's really hi-tech.

Chapter 20

THE REST OF THE STORY

My good friend, State Representative Max Black, refrained from presenting me with the following until 2½ years after I left the Governor's office. He probably thought I'd be embarrassed.

To the contrary I'm happy that he so poignantly pointed out the frailties of a busy Governor. He properly called it "The Rest of the Story." Here is Representative Black's report:

"On September 20, 1996, The Arc, a charitable organization, held a ribbon cutting ceremony at the Boise City Mounted Police stables. The occasion celebrated the completion of a community sponsored art project featuring a number of local kids having disabilities. Governor Phil Batt, Mayor Brent Coles and Velma Morrison all were invited to participate in the ceremonies.

The art project was funded by a grant designed to improve the lot of children with disabilities. A well-known local artist, Shannon Fausey, supervised the project and assisted the individual kids in painting a large mural on the wall of a warehouse building .... The mural was titled "Horses of a Different Color." The mural depicted that, like horses, people with disabilities are different but at the same time the same. In addition to a number of differently-colored horses the mural depicted several outbuildings with the self-portraits of some of the kids participating on the project........

As the program progressed, Governor Batt, who at first requested that he not be asked to speak, decided that he had a few comments to offer. As the Governor rose to speak, he walked over to the mural and stopped in front of one of the horses painted on the wall. That horse was going through the barn door with just the back part of the horse showing. The Governor praised the painting in general and congratulated all the kids for their efforts and then pointed to the back of the horse going through the door and said, 'There are some here in the audience that think the end of the horse going into the barn is my self-portrait.' This comment, of course, brought the house down with the kids all having a good laugh. As funny as this comment was at the time, it's the rest of story that needs to be told.

When Governor Batt was first invited to attend the event, some weeks before, the invitation was turned down by his office due to a scheduling conflict ...Representative Black, an Arc board member, contacted the Governor's office to determine whether the Governor could attend if the date or time was changed. He was advised that the Governor could attend earlier in the evening than the original request and if it were understood that he would not be one of the speakers........

The day of the event, Representative Black received a call from Eva Gay Yost, the Governor's scheduler, requesting him to meet the Governor in the parking lot to escort him to the arena and fill him in on the details of the events. Representative Black was reminded that the Governor was not to be asked to speak since he would not have prepared remarks and since this was his fourth event of the day he would be very tired and would want to leave early to go straight home..........

Of course the first person to greet the Governor was the master of ceremonies who immediately asked the Governor if he would like to say a few words. Before Representative Black could react the Governor very curtly replied, "NO!"

As the Governor walked into the arena all of the kids started to jump up and down wanting to get a look at him and shake his hand if they could get close enough. You could see the Governor's heart melt away and he took the time to shake hands with every one of the kids. The start of the program was delayed due to the extended greetings but as it got under way, with both Mayor Coles and Velma Morrison speaking about the participation of all these enthusiastic kids, tears started to well up in the Governor's eyes. He leaned down to Representative Black and asked if he might be allowed to say a few words after all. Governor Batt's words were much better coming from the heart than had he prepared a speech prior to the event.

A couple of days later Representative Black met Eva Gay in the hallway of the Capitol and told her how well Governor Batt had done at the ceremony. This prompted her to ask him what had happened that evening. She said that she had been working late and, suddenly and totally unexpectedly, Governor Batt walked into his office.........Before she could ask him what he was doing there the Governor said, 'Well, I went ahead and spoke at that ribbon cutting!' Eva Gay asked him what he said to them, to which the Governor replied, 'I told them what a horse's behind I was!' With no further explanation he left the office laughing to himself. This left Eva Gay wondering what in the world he meant by that, and what had actually happened."

Self-portrait at Arc. That's me on the left.

Chapter 21

ERIC THE UNWILLING NAZI

Friendships among old folks sometimes pop up in unexpected places. Probably the most fertile of hunting grounds is the golf course.

As previously stated, Jacque and I own a modest winter home in Green Valley, Arizona, 35 miles north of the Mexican border. There are eight courses in or adjacent to Green Valley, and the pastime of choice is golf.

My winter visits were sparse until I retired from politics, so I became accustomed to golfing as a walk-on single. Ninety percent of the time there was no difficulty, and I had the privilege of playing with dozens of different golfers – male and female. They ranged from hackers to those who could shoot their age. They were all good people. Most were from the upper Midwest, but nearly every state was represented, with a sizeable contingent from Canada.

Last winter I was in Green Valley for several months straight, so my outings evolved into a regular foursome. The other three had lost a member and they kindly asked me to join their group.

There is Art, a retired banker from a small city in Iowa. Next is Curt, the youngster of the group at 65. He is a developer, and has homes in San Diego and Green Valley.

Then there is Eric. Eric Kupka is from Vancouver, British Columbia. But you could readily sense from his thick accent that his roots came from somewhere else.

We played a couple of times a week for a good while before I got Eric to open up about his past. We were sharing the same cart when I mentioned my military service in the Big War and that I had enlisted at age 17. The Air Force had delayed calling me to active duty until I became 18 and the atom bomb was dropped while I was still in basic training. The war ended soon after.

From previous conversations I knew that Eric had been born and had grown to adulthood in Germany. He is a couple of years younger than I and would have still been a teenager when the Germans capitulated.

My curiosity got the better of me, and I asked him what the wartime scene was like in Nazi Germany. Eric hesitated, only briefly (I learned later that he hadn't told the others much about his past), but then he began to talk freely about his remarkable story.

Eric Kupka's parents were from upper Silesia which was a part of Germany, bordering on Poland, prior to the onset of World War I. Upon the defeat of Kaiser Wilhelm's regime, part of Silesia was given over to Poland. Eric's father, who had fought in World War I as a 17-year-old German soldier, moved into the remaining German part of Silesia. It was there, in the town of Leobschuets, that Eric was born.

Two days after the Second World War started, Eric's father was again drafted. He fought in both wars!

Then, in December 1944, Eric was also conscripted at the age of 15^1/$_2$. He was training in the mountains of Czechoslovakia when he heard on the radio that his home town had been over-run by the Red Army, amid heavy fighting and casualties. He had no way of finding out what had happened to his mother and sisters. After he was reunited with his family years later, he learned that the German commander ordered the evacuation of the city upon the approach of the Red Army. All civilians, including his family, were loaded on freight trains and moved to the west.

Young men such as Eric were being used as cannon fodder by the unscrupulous Nazi military leaders. Fortunately, the war ended before he saw combat, and he returned home on his sixteenth birthday.

He walked up to his house, and found that it was occupied by Russian soldiers. They had moved all the furniture out on the lawn and filled the house with cots, converting it into Russian barracks.

Eric is a fairly small man and the Russian Commander did not view him as a soldier. As a result, he escaped arrest and confinement. Instead, this teenage German was ordered to serve as an errand boy for the occupying troops. The Commander liked him, and he was given a variety of chores, including caring for the horses.

One day Eric was taking the horses down to a nearby watering trough. A long line of captured German soldiers filed by. The horses fidgeted as one POW approached. He sported a large flowing beard, and he looked ominous as he approached Eric. Suddenly, the big man lifted Eric into the air and asked, "Who is your mother?"

Only then did Eric recognize his father, who had been captured earlier. Even this dire situation was a relief because he had had no previous knowledge of what happened to either his father or his mother.

The father was to remain a prisoner in a nearby camp for another year, and was forced to work repairing railroad tracks. Because of the location of those duties, he managed to smuggle Eric on a refugee train bound for West Germany at the end of 1946. There, with the help of the Red Cross, he found his mother and sister. His mother died about 6 months later at the age of 43. His father was not released until 1950 but was then allowed to join his children.

After the defeat of the Nazis in World War II, the remaining part of Silesia and other territories were ceded to Poland. This was to make up for territories taken from Poland by Russia on the eastern side.

Eric Kupka decided that he had no desire to return to his native homeland which was no longer part of Germany.

To quote Eric: "I finished my education—chemistry—but I was not happy. I had lost my homeland; my father had lost his homeland not only once, but twice in his lifetime. I decided that if I wanted a future for myself and any possible family, it

Eric Kupka, Hamburg, Germany (1954), "Turning my back on Germany."

had to be somewhere else. So I began to make plans for emigration. My first choice of countries was America, but with very few exceptions, the U.S. did not take any German immigrants. However, Canada, a country I knew nothing about, was looking for people. So I found myself at the end of 1952 with $25 in my pocket, on an old converted troop transport ship en route to Halifax, Nova Scotia. While crossing the Atlantic I made myself two promises: 1. No matter how bad things might turn out, I would never go back, except for a visit. 2. I will become a good citizen of my newly adopted country. I kept both my promises.

I met Trudy, who is Austrian, in Toronto, where we got married."

73

Eric Kupka's new life (1957), Toronto, Canada. A beautiful woman (Trudy), a great country (Canada), "What more does one man want?"

He subsequently moved around his beloved Canada to take advantage of opportunities within his company. The last move settled him near Vancouver, a long trek from Nova Scotia.

He is a happy man. He makes friends easily and does his best to please all comers. But Eric Kupka still reflects the tensions of his troubled past. Although he condemns the brutal and senseless terrorist attacks on the United States, he's inclined to view President Bush as a bit of a bully. Like Rodney King, he wishes everybody would "just get along" and there would be no more wars.

Eric and Trudy Kupka, 45 years together in Canada.

Chapter 22

CATS THAT GO BUMP
IN THE NIGHT

There are these friends of mine who live out in the country near the place I farmed for most of my working life. I won't say who they are, or whether they are related to me, because I don't want any unfortunate repercussions to befall me for relating this tale.

This fine family has two cats. One is a large, well-rounded long-haired beauty named MR. CAT. The other, a runty alleycat type female with bulls-eye markings on its sides has been labeled Bobbicat.

The cats are fairly normal in daylight hours, but at night they play out cat fantasies. Because of loud humping and thumping noises interrupting their sleep, my friends began placing the cats in separate rooms of the house during nocturnal hours.

The Lord of the house, whom I shall refer to as Master, pretends to loathe the cats, but is actually quite fond of them.

He shares the same problem of most other men; he often needs to relieve himself once or more during the nighttime. They leave the bedroom door ajar at a certain aperture so that Master will not become disoriented in the dark.

But one fateful night MR. CAT, during his meanderings, bumped the door and caused it to hang at an unfamiliar angle.

When Master rose for his usual chore, he charged right into the edge of the door, causing a loud crash and a sore cranium.

MR. CAT, who is spooky by nature, fled the scene at full speed, careening into an open screen door leading to the patio. He warped the screen and entangled himself in it.

Master, in trying to extricate MR. CAT, accidentally loosed Bobbicat from her resting place and she joined in the melee. The screen door collapsed onto the deck with a deafening roar. Bobbicat and MR. CAT both fled into the darkness, MR. CAT's large fluffy tail flashing in the moonlight.

MR. CAT on the telephone calling out the Fat Cat Brigade.

Bobbicat, an accessory to the crime.

The Master of the house finally made it back to bed, muttering loudly, "That lard-ass cat has got to go." Of course he won't. They need him. Entertainment opportunities are not plentiful out in the country.

But MR. CAT was taking no chances. When he and Bobbicat finally appeared at noon the next day, he carefully laid a dead mouse on the doorstep.

Epilogue:

The Mistress of the house has now taken in two more strays. One, incredibly, survived a 200-mile fishing trip by riding up in the wheel well of their pickup. They went through mud puddles deep enough to cover the door sills, with brush scraping the bottom most of the way. Needless to say, that cat is spooky. The other is fairly dense but nice and tame.

Understandably, Master says enough is enough. The two new cats are confined to my office in Wilder where the mice no longer have it made.

Chapter 23

AN EDELWEISS CHRISTMAS STORY

My friend Jerry Deckard prides himself on having a rather rough exterior. But inside he's a man of compassion and sophistication. Jerry is a dedicated proponent of self-improvement and nowhere does he practice that pursuit more religiously than on the golf course.

Deckard has a powerful upper body. He takes a short backswing and a mighty swat at the ball. He gave up his woods long ago because of their erratic behavior. But, if everything goes right, he can hit a 3-iron tee shot 225 yards.

It doesn't always go right.

We have this mutual friend, Bill Deal, who knows how to play the game. He often scores in the 70s. And, even better, he always seems content with whatever he shoots. He's that rarity of rarities - a man who is happy with his golf game. He's serene.

Deckard has this overwhelming desire to play golf like Bill. So he asked him for his secret.

Bill said, "Jerry, if you really want to know, I'll tell you. You need to have a harmonious attitude when you hit the ball. On your backswing, sing to yourself 'Edelweiss' with an upward inflection. Then, on the down stroke do the same, only with the descending phrase—like this: Ed-el-weiss, Ed-el-weiss."

Jerry tried it. It was a miracle. He was hitting the ball like a demon.

He could hardly wait for the weekly outing with our regular golfing group. He told us of his remarkable improvement and sang regularly for us - Edelweiss, Edelweiss, over and over.

In fact, Mr. Deckard did very well for the first three holes. But then, suddenly, the Alpine magic disappeared. He stubbed several shots, in spite of frantic singing.

But he was still confident. He stepped to the tee, trolled off "Edelweiss," and took a vigorous swing. The ball sailed out of bounds. One of the wise guys piped up, "Hey, Jerry, we're gonna' have to bring Julie Andrews over to sing Adel-vise." Deckard glowered, teed up another ball, and quickly sent it in pursuit of the other one. Out-of-bounds.

"It's gonna' take the whole damn Von Trapp family," he dejectedly concluded.

Maybe so, but we're all thinking of the Swiss Alps when we hit the ball these days. It's helped our scores a little and it makes my Christmas shopping easier. I'm getting Jerry Deckard a CD soundtrack from the "Sound of Music."

Chapter 24

A PEARL OF PEARLS

I shared the shock and disbelief that overwhelmed all Americans when hate-filled sadists slammed their hijacked airplanes into New York's twin towers and the Pentagon. Except for the heroic actions of passengers, a fourth plane would probably have taken out the nation's Capitol or the White House.

Even though news agencies did an excellent job of bringing the agonizing personal stories of many of the 3,000 victims to light, it was natural to think of them collectively, instead of mourning each as a tragic victim of senseless slaughter.

That's why the torture and beheading of reporter Daniel Pearl seemed to hit me even harder. The first chilling e-mail pictures of that handsome young man with a gun held to his head riveted my attention. I could think of little else. I prayed to God that he would take me, an old man, and let Danny live. But I had little hope from the start.

Then I began to wonder. Do I pray to the same God as Danny Pearl? He was a Jew and probably did not believe that God and Jesus Christ and the Holy Spirit are all one entity. My Mother used to think that Jews and Mormons might be good people but they'd likely face obstacles toward making it to heaven.

But all that hairsplitting did not and does not concern me. My personal God welcomes all who are kind and helpful to one another and who acknowledge their sins.

After all, there are billions and billions of people on this earth who are not Christians. In fact there are at least a billion who do not believe in any God.

Some say that Christianity has encouraged violence against non-believers, especially during the crusades. By a convoluted twisting of the Scriptures a Christian might excuse that behavior, but I've never met one who does. Certainly there are fanatics in all religions but any person who was perverted enough to kill in the name of Christ would be condemned by nearly all other Christians. My personal Lord and Savior demands that I confess (and be forgiven) if I would personally wish physical harm to anyone. The very thought of it is anti-Christian.

Not so with some extremist Muslims. I presume that the vast majority of Muslims are outraged by the recent terrorist insanity, yet authorities in Muslim nations have said little or nothing that is critical of their murdering Al-Quida brethren. School children in Muslim countries are taught to hate America in the name of their religion. Some things that have gone on in those mosques, even in this country, have been inimical to the safety and well-being of this free and tolerant nation. I don't believe that kind of religion has the blessing of a just God or Allah.

I don't know if I will be denied entry to the pearly gates because I can't maintain the belief that only Christians, exclusively, are given eternal life. Almighty God will make those decisions and I pray that I will be included.

84

But, if Danny and I don't make it there, I hope I will spend my afterlife in another venue with him. Mr. Pearl was a decent, caring husband and reporter – a happy man who played the violin and wished no harm to anyone. Yet, because he was a Jew, he was butchered by fiends who will surely burn in hell.

Chapter 25

TIME FLIES – CHANGE FLIES FASTER

It is universally agreed that the years go by far too quickly. One year piles into the next and, the first thing you know, you've grown much older.

But it's not like changing events have fallen behind this pace. My father and my mother were born before Idaho became a state, and my grandfather was born while this noble experiment, called the United States of America, was still in its first century. I have lived almost exactly one-third of the entire existence of this blessed country.

The changes we have undergone are mind-boggling, and the process of change accelerates with each passing year. The Wright brothers took their first tottering flight in 1903. Less than 60 years later, President Kennedy promised that we would put a man on the moon within 10 years, and we did.

Electronic communication dazzles the imagination. From the inspired early efforts of Bell, Marconi, and others, we can now reach virtually anyone in the world within moments. Yet, it seems that we had better be careful what we say across this planet, as technicians are able to reconstruct phone messages and e-mails after they are transmitted and deleted.

Breakthroughs in health care have added almost 20 years to our lifespans over the past half-century.

Modern technology has also produced weapons of war which can annihilate millions of people in a few terrible moments. Unrest has not eased with scientific advancement. Man's penchant for cruelty to man continues on, unabated and seems to intensify each year.

Inventions and innovations have made housework, homework, farming, and manufacturing easier. They have given us a wide array of leisure choices and a panorama of educational opportunities.

Yes, we live in exciting times.

What useful, maybe fearsome, maybe cataclysmic, changes will occur during the next century? We have not had too much luck with predicting the future and, I suspect, we will be less accurate as the pace of change accelerates.

It must be disheartening to young folks to see the degenerate, senseless turmoil created throughout the world by all types of fanatics. It seems as if the majority of these uncivilized acts are committed in the name of religion.

My God is a just God and He will surely show us how to turn accelerating change into a more beneficial pattern in the near future.

Chapter 26

HIGH NOON – THE HAPPY HOUR

I've never spent a summer in Green Valley, Arizona. It's hot – temperatures of 110 degrees are not that rare and, with the exception of the monsoon rains of late summer, there are only occasional days of relief from the searing heat.

But people adapt and geezers, who have become experts at coping with changing circumstances throughout their lives, take it all in stride.

Even in the winter, most Green Valleyans are up before 6 a.m. Conversely they roll up the sidewalks when the sun goes down. The only excitement that happens at night is accidental, such as the time the firemen evacuated a nursing home because of smoke billowing out. But it was nothing more sinister than popcorn burning in a microwave oven.

The evening hours are great for shopping at the local grocery store. The ordinarily rude shoppers have gone to bed and you can traverse the aisle without some big lady ramming you with her cart.

Those who stay the year 'round in Green Valley tell me that this shift toward the early hours is much more pronounced in the hot summer season. The good old dog is happy to go for his walk at 4 a.m. Many golfers play every day, with 6 a.m. tee times at a premium.

Prime time for dinner reservations gravitates toward 4:30 p.m. in the summer. The restaurants do a good business because it's pretty hot to barbecue at home.

Well then, what to do about happy hour? The usual 5 p.m. to 7 p.m. time slot certainly doesn't fit. But that's no reason to foreswear the conviviality that comes with the time-honored tradition of happy hours.

None of the Green Valley bars start the time of cut-rate libation later than 3 p.m., but the Arizona Café is the champion. A large sign proclaims that happy hour at that fine eatery starts at high noon – and everyone has a high old time!

Chapter 27

A SCARY ART SAFARI

My wife Jacque has a real eye for art. She is talented and tasteful in appraising aesthetic items and has collected paintings and other art objects all of our married life. She has also preserved several pieces of handiwork from her forbears.

Tubac is an art colony 20 miles south of our winter home. The village was established in 1752, the first permanent European (Spanish) settlement in the region. It encompasses several historic buildings including an ancient mission and an early military fort. The story of its colorful past is fascinating, but the most popular attraction is the wide variety of art on display. Many of those who create these interesting pieces are residents of the town. Others come in periodically to sell their wares.

Several shops serve as the conduit between artist and buyer. I am comfortable in most of these places but the fancier ones cause me some anxiety.

Jacque loves Tubac and can easily spend a half day browsing among the offerings. I tag along or do a crossword puzzle while sitting on the benches outside those high-class purveyors of creative works.

Tubac art is unique and exotic.

One art salon there is a cut above the others with its unique offerings. They are really expensive so I usually stay out, but on one occasion I followed Jacque into the shop. While she was looking at some paintings I tiptoed around the gallery.

There was an interesting collection of terra cotta and metal shapes and designs in one section. Several fake animals and figurines sat in close proximity. I became fascinated by a giant rooster. It was multi-colored and carried a bedazzling price tag of $1,800. I couldn't resist tipping it a bit to get a better look at its tail.

Suddenly the tail became entangled with the arms of an Aztec warrior. The entire exhibit leaned precariously. I broke out in a nervous sweat and gingerly attempted to free the rooster. It appeared that if I applied enough pressure I would likely break part of its tail off.

I was ready to give up and call Jacque or the proprietor or both, but was afraid to let loose for fear of damage to the goods. The Lord intervened and the statuettes parted. Of course, I was studiously appraising something else when those two reappeared.

Chapter 28

HOW OLD IS OLD?

A Governor gets asked to a wide variety of events. If there's a funeral for a cat you will likely be asked to give the eulogy.

Nearly all these potential scheduled events are interesting – some much more than others. As I was not the youngest Governor, I guess I had a bias toward events that featured older people.

When a certain authority (I don't remember who) was asked, "How old is old?" he replied, "Old is 20 years older than you are." This would translate into a range of about 90 years of age when I was in office.

Well, two of my favorite appointments during my gubernatorial tenure involved women of the age of 94 years and 104 years respectively.

The 94-year-old was my former fourth grade teacher and I called on her in her Meridian assisted-living home to help her celebrate her birthday.

I didn't think Ms. McConaughey looked much different than she did 60 years ago when I was a kid and she was about 30 but, after all, my own perspective was different then – all adults looked old.

We had a great visit. Reporters were there. They asked her if I had been a well-behaved student. The old gal lied and said that I had applied myself diligently, performed admirably and was well-behaved. I looked back on my report card and, under deportment, she had written 'needs improvement.' Time heals all things.

The birthday for the 104-year-old was a large gala affair. Ethel McArthur was brought into the reception room of the Life Care Center of Idaho. She looked fabulous and could easily have passed for someone much younger.

Ethel McArthur's 104th birthday party.

Ms. McConaughey (at top) and my 4th grade class. I'm holding #71, and I thought she looked mighty old.

Ethel was profoundly deaf, but otherwise sharp as a tack. Those attending her would write their message or question on a pad and shout into her ear and she would sometimes respond. She had not yet figured out who I was until her aide wrote "Governor Batt" on her pad. "GOVERNOR!" she bellowed. She had no idea of the volume in her voice.

We cut the cake and had a merry time. I had brought her a memento from my office with my name etched into a weighty plastic paperweight. She examined it carefully. There was no comment for a few minutes. Then she let out a mighty roar, "IT'S HEAVY – SMALL, BUT HEAVY!" Ethel looked mighty pleased. I was mighty pleased. After all, my staff members had made a fetish of denigrating the "glass chunks" I used for such an occasion. I had proven my superior wisdom to those young upstarts.

Back to the festivities. At the appropriate time they started the music. It was a boogie type recording. A 90-year-old, who had appeared rather lethargic in her wheelchair, sprang to her feet and started doing a vigorous twist. It was a good celebration. Ms. McArthur has now passed on. I'm glad I got to go to her party.

Chapter 29

DISCRIMINATION ON THE GREENBELT

Among Boise's treasures, none is more valuable than the Greenbelt. This river walkway allows those of us with rural roots to enjoy a natural scene without traveling to the country. And the urban natives enjoy it just as much.

It's there that you can observe raccoons sneaking along the bank looking for duck eggs, see and hear all kinds of birds and spot an occasional deer. The tree-covered setting exerts a calming sensation. It is the ideal place for dog-walking or pulling a tot in a wagon behind a bicycle.

But the weirdo freaks in our society prevent the Greenbelt from being a place of equal opportunity. Most women are chary of walking along the river alone, especially in the late evening, and few would attempt it at night.

This points out again that the male of the human species leaves a lot to be desired. I don't ever recall hearing of a man being assaulted or murdered on the Greenbelt, and, if a woman has ever perpetrated a Greenbelt crime, it's news to me.

The creeps that prey upon women and children are cowards. They do their despicable deeds in the dark or in a secluded spot. They are the rotten dregs of society. They are condemned by all normal people and provide the best argument for the death penalty.

Most of us men would gladly throw the switch that would fry a molester. Yet we much admit that such behavior is almost totally a male aberration.

Why? I don't know. All we can do is be vigilant – prevent these events when possible; punish severely those sickies who are caught; and protect our women and children at all costs.

Chapter 30

THIS WHITE ELEPHANT IS A KEEPER

I waited far too long to get into volunteer work at Green Valley, my winter home. My excuse was that my residency there was too intermittent to make me a reliable volunteer. That was only partially true.

Jacque started in the volunteer business before I did by taking our dog to visit elderly patients in the nursing homes. There is a regular day for this. Nearly all of the residents are very ill and some don't want a dog making up to them, but most are delighted and, Nessie, urged on by her irrepressible Mistress, is a big hit. I sometimes go along and coax my show-off dog into more tom-foolery.

But that's irrelevant, as I found my niche in the volunteer business last winter at no other place than a second-hand store.

The White Elephant is a thrift store with the net proceeds going to a variety of charities determined by a local board.

It has been in operation for about 20 years and started as a comparatively small operation. Annual production of charitable proceeds reached $100,000 only a few years ago. Last year

Mr. Clean workin' at the White Elephant. "I can really make those floors shine!"

the take was about a million dollars and this year looks better yet.

There are several reasons behind the success of this venture. The elderly population provides quality used merchandise due to the death or disablement of a substantial number of residents annually.

The board of directors is aggressive and completed a successful drive to greatly enlarge the facility recently. It is now a huge edifice carrying everything from soup to nuts.

But the main factor that has propelled the growth of the White Elephant is the outstanding group of volunteers that staff it daily. There are about 160 of these highly dedicated workers. It is a social plus to work at the White Elephant in our small retirement city and the store is probably the number one topic of conversation in town except, perhaps, the library.

Most "employees" serve one or two days a week and they give it their all. Receiving people start in the wee hours to ready the store for its daily influx of materials. Salespersons start about 8 a.m. and work well past the noon closing time. Delivery persons work all day hauling the goods to anyplace from the Mexican border to Tucson.

There are daily volunteer supervisors who start about 5 a.m. When I stepped up to the plate my boss, Bill, handed me a broom and told me to get with it. It takes me about an hour and a half to sweep that gigantic floor, but I did it on Tuesday and sometimes on other days all winter.

Bill also gave me my big chance. He was short of salesmen and started me out in the used furniture section. There I had the honor of hawking all sorts of furniture from elegant to bizarre. We sold 3-legged stools and we sold $1500 organs.

For one with no experience along this line, I did okay. My political background put me at ease with potential buyers, as well as stoically accepting the "no sales" that often come after tantalizing interest is demonstrated.

At first I was sloppy with my paperwork and it took several chewing-outs from my fellow workers before I got it down to a science.

When I return to Green Valley this fall, I will immediately apply for another chance to be part of the venture. I can't wait to sucker some other snowbird into buying an ugly green chair even if we have to cut the price – we do that after 10 days on the floor with no takers. And I look forward, equally, to sweeping those spacious floors. You can really tell that you're getting something done.

Chapter 31

STOMPING AT THE STAMP

One of the advantages of being a Geezer is that you can recall events of the past with little fear of contradiction. Most of my friends from the 3-cent stamp days have died off, so I can safely take some literary license with this breathtaking tale of postal history.

I remember well the era of the 3-cent first-class letter postal rate. It seems like it lasted forever. I suppose there was a time when 2-cents or 1-cent would suffice to send a letter but, if I ever knew about it, I've blocked that period out of my mind as irrelevant. 3-cents was the perfect charge.

During the rise from 3-cents to 37-cents, I only know that the postal service has strived mightily to cope with a mushrooming responsibility. It has had to compete with an avalanche of improvements in telephones, faxes, e-mails, etc. Except for spamming, delivery of most of the worthless junk mail messages remains the responsibility of the U.S. Postal Service. Yet the public demands that first-class mail be delivered on time, at a reasonable cost.

I have found the employees to be a dedicated, helpful lot who do not seem to mind working through a complicated mailing process for which the Postal Service receives only a pittance.

My wife, Jacque, likes the Post Office employees, too. However, she views the Service as a mysterious organization that is out to bedevil one's life with postage stamp increases. Jacque collected stamps for a long time and still has a good, but inactive, assortment. But that is a separate matter from coping with real live postage needs. Just as she settles into a balanced supply and demand situation with her stamps, the price is raised and her remaining stock-on-hand is obsolete.

I like to bring her little surprises, and I sometimes fetch home a pane or a 100-count sheet of a new issue. She is delighted, but she's inclined to shuffle them around so that quite a few are left over when the next raise occurs.

Thus, when I inventoried her active stamp supply, I found the following:

(a) Two kinds of 1-centers, with an American kestrel and an omnibus from the 1880's featured. The 1-centers are the most useful of the lot because, in company with another stamp, they can reach any legal threshold. However, if too many are used (like 37) there's no room left for the address;

(b) A 3-center with a Conestoga wagon, but none from the era when it counted;

(c) A 4-cent steam carriage;

(d) A 5-cent circus wagon;

(e) A whole bunch of 10-cent canal boat stamps – why the surplus is unknown.

(f) We skip up to 20-cents. Were there few raises in the interim? I leave it to other researchers to solve this mystery. (There was a 19-cent postcard also – current? I doubt it.)

(g) 23-cents – Now we're getting back in the groove. This one depicted a nice lunch wagon.

(h) 32-cents – Wow! What a leap. If my memory serves me correctly that 32-cents postage for a letter lasted a long time. It emboldened me to bring home large numbers of stamps. Some that are left are of Santa Claus, the Statue of Liberty, and the U.S. flag – all bastions of stability – also a Corsair airplane, toy fish, toy squirrels and a stratojet.

(i) But that era had to end also, and the 33-center came along. I bought too many and we now have berries and fruits languishing on the table, but a few singles will make them useful. A pile of stamped envelopes also requires augmentation.

(j) The 34-cents quickly followed. I bought 100 of the flowers and 25 of the fruits – bad move.

(k) And so today, we are at 37-cents. I wasn't going to buy any, but who can resist those beautiful Audubon birds. I bought only 60.

We'll probably have them for years to come. They'll add color to Jacque's stash. I still don't understand why she has three $1 stamps in there. They are of foxes and they are sly. Now you see them and then you don't. They disappear among the papers on the table. I'll bet they're waiting for first-class rates to reach the dollar mark. It may not be too long.

Chapter 32

A DEBIT DUMBKOFF

It was time to take our annual trek to San Francisco. We haven't made it every one of our 54 years together but we haven't missed very many either.

There have been a lot of changes in "Baghdad at the Bay" over five decades, but some things remain constant, such as an absolute tolerance for bizarre behavior from the eclectic mix of residents of that metropolis.

An even more enduring feature of the city is its uncanny ability to wring large sums of money out of tourists.

I was scheduled to leave on August 2. Jacque left a day early, on the first, in order to get in some extra shopping. My 16-year-old granddaughter, Anna, was to take the plane down with me so that she could feel the flavor of the city for the first time.

I knew it would take a bulging billfold to handle our threesome, so I went down to the trusty automatic teller machine. I've previously stated that I marvel at how these cornucopias of cash operate so accurately.

But, even so, it takes at least a minor amount of brains from the human being operating the ATM, in order to complete the transaction.

I put in my debit card, punched in the numbers, and impatiently waited for the machine to give me the loot. Nothing happened for a while. Then the apparatus spit out my card.

I tried again and this time the monitor read "your card has expired" before regurgitating the plastic. I looked, and sure enough my debit card had expired the day before, on July 31.

Here I was, at 6 p.m. on Friday afternoon, due to board a plane to San Francisco the next morning. The banks were closed.

Well, I called a friend who came down to the bank. He withdrew some cash from the ATM. I wrote him a check. Anna and I got on the plane and joined Grandma and a high old time was had by all at great expense.

After I returned I went to see my banker, Mary Panzeri. Mary is a wonderful lady who may have a cold banker's heart but I've never seen her display it. I asked for a new debit card. She had me fill out the forms and said she would expedite it, but then she said, "I can't understand why you didn't get your renewal card."

She showed me her new one and then the awful truth dawned on me. The new card was a multi-colored upscale model. The old one was dull and drab.

I remembered then that I had received a flashy new card in the mail. Thinking it was another credit card promotion, I quickly moved into action. "I need another card like I need another hole in my head," I said, "I'll show those promoters." I snatched up a pair of scissors, snipped the card in two, and threw it in the wastebasket.

The new debit card came through in speedy fashion, just as my banker had promised. "Now is the time to snip up the old one," I thought. Evidently another senior moment set in as you'll soon see.

As I had stockpiled some cash, I had no immediate use for new funds. It was three weeks later that my billfold was depleted and I went to the ATM. I stuck in my card, and confidently went through the procedures. "Your card has expired," was the cryptic message. I looked at it and it was the same old useless card I had tried before.

Had I scissored the new one again? It was not in my billfold. I could picture myself getting on my knees and begging my banker lady for a new one. I'm used to having to do that for a farm loan but not for a debit card.

Ten days later the new card showed up under the seat of my car where I had spilled all the cards out of my billfold one day.

Now I have the old one lying in front of me on the table. It's failed me twice in my time of need. I have my scissors at hand and that card is going to get it. Now, if I can just decide if it's the right one.

Final

A 75-YEAR INVENTORY

In my book "The Compleat Phil Batt," I reprinted a column I wrote for the weeklies in 1977. The column was entitled "Living 5 Decades," and was a summary of goals that I had reached at age 50 as well as those that I had hoped to attain in the future.

That column promised another inventory at age 75. Well, I'm already there. "O, Time in thy relentless flight!"
Here I go!

At 50 I said: I've picked up as many beer cans along the road as I threw out before I got to know better.

At 75: I no longer pick up beer cans along the road although I continue to pack them out of the Owyhee Mountain campsites where I pursue the wily trout. I believe cleaning the highway barrow pits of debris is a fitting sentence for those convicted of minor offenses.

At 50: I've helped carry more persons to the grave than it will take to carry me.

At 75: If I'm asked to be a pallbearer these days I'm classed as "honorary." The young folks carry the casket and I'm glad to be relieved of that chore. I didn't want to be seen as shoving my share of the work onto the big guys, so I strove mightily to do my share of the lifting.

At 50: I've cleaned more fish than I'll ever eat.
At 75: I still clean fish.

At 50: I've milked my share of cows and mowed the requisite number of lawns.
At 75: No cow milking or lawn mowing.

At 50: I was calling on as many old people as I want to call on me when I'm old.
At 75: I'm still calling on old folks, some of whom are younger than I am.

At 50: I was determined to plant as many trees as I've cut down.
At 75: No more tree planting. However, I plant all the shrubs and flowers that Jacque brings home. I hate it when the garden stores have sales.

At 50: I attempted to lift my family's spirits as many times as they have lifted mine.
At 75: I'm still working on lifting my family's spirits. I must confess to being the depressant at times.

At 50: I tried to write as many thank-yous as needed to be written.
At 75: I still do pretty well on the thank yous. I'm amazed that people are so thoughtful of me.

At 50: One of my goals was shooting better golf than former Governor Andrus.
At 75: I can beat my friend Cecil Andrus on the golf course more times than not. I'm on a hot streak and he hasn't

much time for practice. He is still an accomplished haggler, so I cave in and give him too many strokes.

At 50: Another goal: Attempt to smile more times than I frown.

At 75: I smile more times than I frown.

At 50: A goal: Attempt to stay in good physical shape.

At 75: I'm in good shape for a 75-year old. My dog requires incessant walking.

At 50: I want to learn to accept criticism easier; to listen better; to give the opinions of my political opponents fair consideration (this one will be hard).

At 75: Blah, blah, blah. Who wants to accept criticism easier – or listen better – or give other opinions fair consideration? These were foolish concessions and I no longer worry about them.

The difference in my attitude compared to 25 years previous is easy to spot. At fifty I was predicating my opinions and actions on the future. Now I'm looking backward, reflecting on the past and enjoying it. That's why I chose to end my governorship at one term. I wanted some time to sum up my life. It was a good and proper move.

I'm not planning another inventory when I'm 100 years old. Yet, I can truthfully say that I'm weathering the onslaught of old age pretty well. The body can go to pot any time but hasn't yet. I'm playing golf and playing my clarinet better than I ever have.

Celebrating my 50th birthday in the Idaho Senate chambers.

People treat me with more deference than I deserve. I get to keep score for the golf game and that usually nets me a dollar or two.

Friends and acquaintances and strangers alike engage me in wonderful conversations, ignoring the fact that I can't hear part of it and that I don't keep up my end of the patter. All in all, life as a Geezer is treating me well.

116